The Adventures of Pegadon

Overcoming Bullying

Book 01

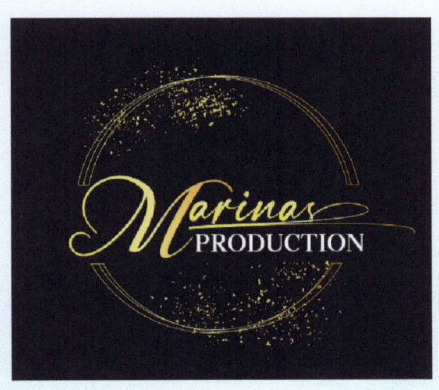

Marinas PRODUCTION

Marina Kalendareva

Illustrated by
Ishani Samarathunga

The Adventures of Pegadon
Marina Kalendareva
Instagram - @kidsareourblessing

Copyright © 2022, 2024
First Edition Published 2022
Marina Kalendareva

ISBN - 979-8-9875258-1-4
Fiction
Library of Congress Cataloging-in-Publication Data

Dedicated to all my nieces and nephews and most of all my beautiful children Evelyn and Noah.

Long, long ago, in the Kingdom of Animals far away, lived two very good friends. Their names were Noah, the Pegasus horse, and Evelyn, the Water dragon.

2

They both had big and mighty wings, which they used to fly high up in the sky! Everyday, the other animals in the Kingdom made fun of Noah and Evelyn because they looked different from the rest of the animals.

They called them all sorts of names and teased them too. "A horse with wings looks so silly," a little rabbit would say and the other animals would laugh.

5

Noah, the Pegasus horse felt sad. His only friend was Evelyn, the Water dragon. The other animals in the Kingdom also made fun of her. "Why are you so big?" a little cat said to Evelyn, and the animals around her laughed. But Evelyn never said anything back.

Every morning, Noah and Evelyn met at the top of the highest mountain. They liked to go there so no one would make fun of them.

"I got teased again because of my wings," Noah said. "Maybe I should find a way to hide them," he added. "No way! A bird was mean to me too, but it's who I am" Evelyn said. "Don't forget who you are, Noah."

All of a sudden, a strange smell and loud thunder was coming from nearby. "Did you hear that?" Noah asked. They both turned to where the noise was coming from.

There was a big fire in the King-dom and the animals were screaming! Noah and Evelyn flew down as fast as they could to help.

Evelyn, the Water dragon, flew towards the fire and began spitting water to put it out. Noah, the Pegasus horse flew down and helped the animals near the fire.

13

14

Noah carried the animals on his back and flew them to a safer place. He then quickly returned to save the rest of the animals that were in danger.

Both Evelyn and Noah worked so hard to put out the fire and bring all the animals to safety. And finally, the Kingdom of Animals was saved!

All of the animals clapped and cheered for them. "Well done! The Pegadon saved us!" they said. "Pegadon?" Evelyn asked. "Yes, the Pegasus and the Dragon," the animals replied.

Pegadon?

The animals apologized for how they treated them in the past and never made fun of them again. From that day on, all of the animals learned to respect one another, even those animals that appeared different from the rest.

Since the Pegadon showed tremendous bravery and courage, all of the creatures in the Kingdom of Animals decided that their land will now be called Pegadonia!

This meant that any and all animals, from all walks of life, from all over the world, can live together in peace and harmony; no matter what they looked like!

23

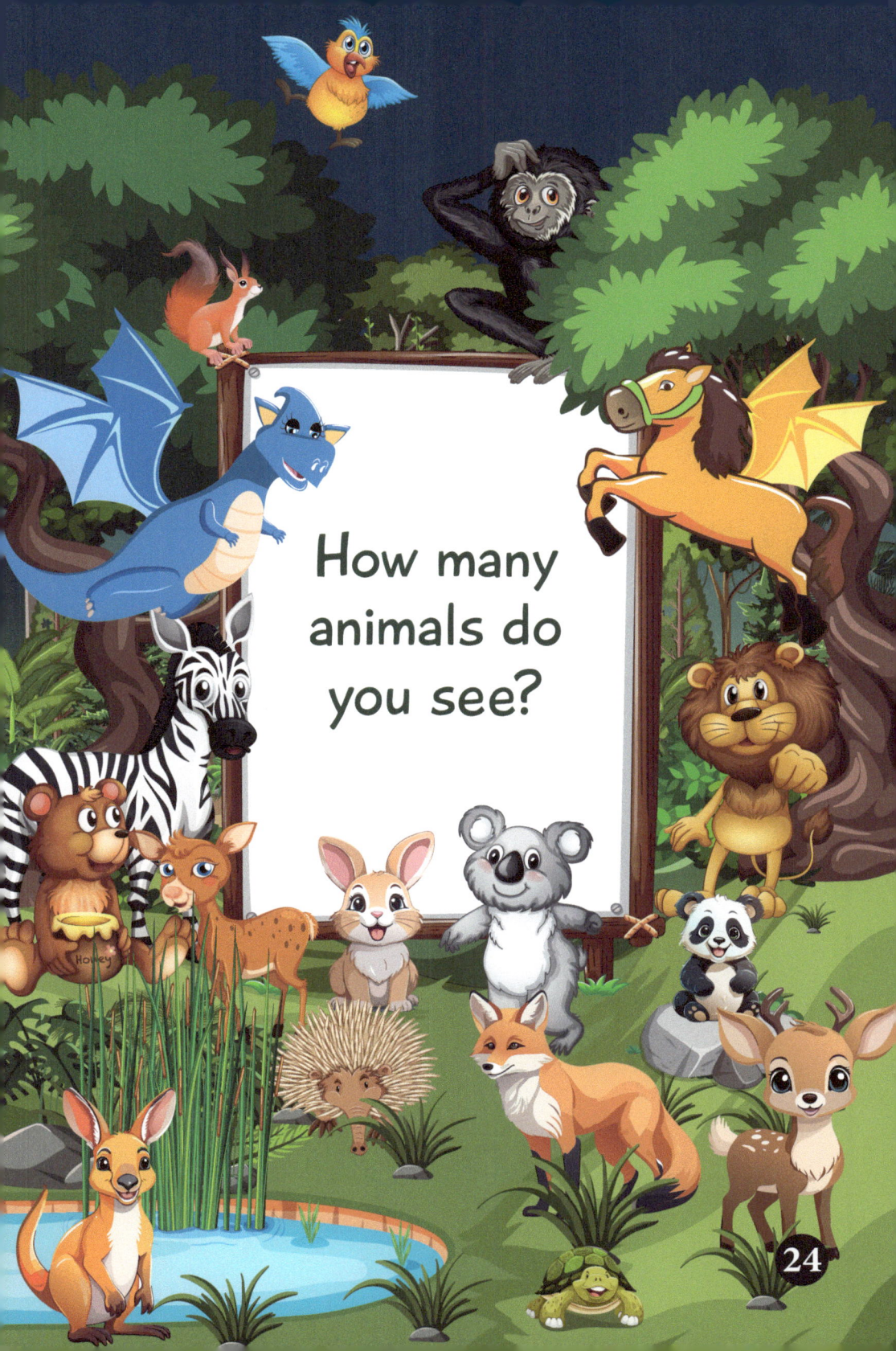

How many animals do you see?

24

I would like to give my gratitude to my family for their support and extend a special thanks to Margarita Kalendareva and Liliya Kalendareva for their invaluable assistance in editing my story to perfection.

I am sincerely grateful to each of them for their unwavering support and contribution to my project.